KATI'S TINY MESSENGERS

MESSENGERS

DR. KATALIN KARIKÓ AND THE BATTLE AGAINST COVID-19

Written by Megan Hoyt
Illustrated by Vivien Mildenberger

Quill Tree Books
An Imprint of HarperCollinsPublishers

Katalin Karikó huddled around the old sawdust stove with her sister, Zsuzsanna. Winters were cold in Hungary, and the wind whipped through the thatched roof of their family's one-room house. They had no TV and no running water, and there was never enough money for candy or toys, but the girls didn't mind. They made up stories about the clucking chickens and snorting pigs and played imaginary games until the pink-orange sun sank over the fields.

Winter turned to spring and spring to summer. When autumn arrived, Mama announced that it was time to go to school.

Kati loved school! Year after year, she pored over her textbooks until the world of science opened before her, like a table spread with diagrams and equations and experiments instead of food.

To Kati, science was fascinating—especially the human body. She closed her eyes and pictured all the systems working together like a well-run machine with millions of tiny parts. She learned how each human cell takes its orders from the command center floating inside its goopy cytoplasm— the nucleus. And how the tiniest workers inside the human body—proteins, enzymes, and chemical compounds—keep a healthy body running smoothly.

Kati's mind raced as she turned each page of her books. She studied hard every night, until Mama turned off the lamp beside her bed and her eyes finally fluttered closed.

But Kati never stopped thinking about science. Even as she slept, questions crashed through her dreams like ocean waves onto the shore.

WHY DO HUMANS SPEAK DIFFERENT LANGUAGES?

WHY DO FINGERNAILS KEEP GROWING BUT EYELASHES DON'T?

WHY DO WE TREMBLE WHEN WE'RE COLD?

WHY DON'T WE CLUCK LIKE CHICKENS OR SNORT LIKE PIGS?

Then, one day she made an important decision.
"I'm going to be a scientist!"
Kati had never even met a scientist. Her father
was a butcher, and her mother was a bookkeeper.
But Kati loved science so much. And once Kati
made a decision, she stuck with it.

Kati studied and studied until she was the top student in her class. She learned about statistics and data and experiments. Finally, it was time to apply to college. Armed with very little money and a heart full of hope, she sent in her applications. And she was accepted to the University of Szegred in Hungary.

The day Kati walked into the science building, she felt lighter than air. She couldn't wait to pursue her dream.

Then her professor started speaking.

In English.

Kati's heart sank. She barely understood basic English. She really only spoke Hungarian. Every time her teachers tried to describe exciting new scientific discoveries, the English words twisted and tangled inside her brain. It took hours to decipher the paragraphs swimming across the pages of her textbooks. But Kati was no quitter. Even if she had to study late into the night. Even if she had to master a whole new language.

Kati crashed through the language barrier and soaked up scientific knowledge like a sponge. She learned about the genetic code inside each cell—called DNA—and about the single strand of messenger RNA (mRNA), all coiled up inside the cell's nucleus like a message inside a bottle, waiting patiently to tell the cell how to behave.

DNA IS A COMPLEX MOLECULE THAT CONTAINS ALL THE INFORMATION NECESSARY to BUILD AND MAINTAIN A LIVING ORGANISM.

ONE ROLE OF RNA IS TO CONVERT THE INFORMATION STORED IN DNA INTO PROTEINS THE CELL CAN USE TO SEND INSTRUCTIONS.

This gave Kati a marvelous idea. What if you could use these messenger strands to teach cells how to fight off dangerous viruses? Maybe deadly diseases could be cured. Kati's heart beat faster, and her face lit up like fireworks across a midnight sky.

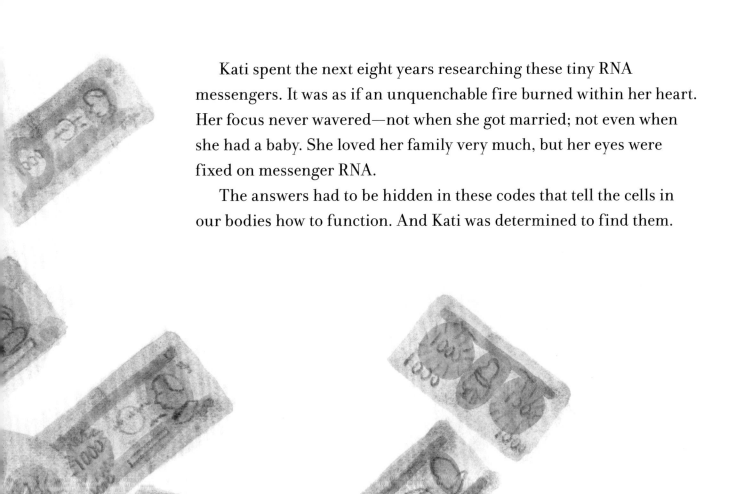

Kati spent the next eight years researching these tiny RNA messengers. It was as if an unquenchable fire burned within her heart. Her focus never wavered—not when she got married; not even when she had a baby. She loved her family very much, but her eyes were fixed on messenger RNA.

The answers had to be hidden in these codes that tell the cells in our bodies how to function. And Kati was determined to find them.

She threw herself into her work.

Then her lab at the university ran out of money.

On her thirtieth birthday, Kati found out she had no job and nowhere to continue her research.

Kati nibbled on her birthday cake, but she barely tasted it. All that studying, all that focus and research—gone.

"If you could do anything in the world right now," her husband, Bela, asked, "what would you choose?"

Kati imagined spotless American labs filled with expert scientists who would work side by side with her and never run out of money.

"I would go to the United States," she said.

Bela nodded. "Then let's go!"

But Hungarian law didn't allow citizens to leave the country
with more than one hundred dollars. That was not enough money
to make a fresh start in a distant country far across the sea.

Kati and Bela stayed up late, jotting down ideas and sharing their dreams for the future while their little daughter, Susan, slept. By morning, they had come up with a daring plan.

Kati packed up their belongings, and Bela sold their car. Then Kati carefully cut open Susan's teddy bear and tucked their savings—around twelve hundred dollars—inside.

Her hands trembled as she stitched the teddy bear closed. Following her dreams required great courage, but she knew her work could save lives one day. She could not give up now.

Life in the United States was hard. Kati worked long hours at a research lab in Philadelphia, performing experiments and carefully recording the data. She was so tired she sometimes fell asleep at her desk. She made very little money, and many experiments ended in failure. But for Kati, the hours flew by in a thrilling whirl of scientific inquiry. And every time an experiment failed, she learned something important.

Kati knew if she could harness the power of messenger RNA, she could teach human cells to disrupt the spread of viruses throughout the body. Diseases would be cured. Lives would be saved. But something was stopping the messengers from getting through.

Meanwhile, Bela fixed broken-down lab equipment for her to use at home, and they never once took a vacation. Little Susan worked hard too—on her schoolwork—until she heard the clink of peanut M&M's hitting the bowl each night. That was Kati's signal—it's time to take a break.

But Kati's mind never took a break. Messenger RNA danced through her dreams and filled up her days. She loved her research, even though some scientists were skeptical of her ideas. "This sounds almost like science fiction!" they said. Kati knew it sounded impossible. She had trouble convincing any lab to give her grant money to continue working on these tiny messengers that would tell human cells how to fight viral invaders. But each experiment brought glimmers of hope. She jotted down notes and figures and celebrated every success, no matter how small.

Then she met someone who was as excited about fighting diseases with messenger RNA as she was—Dr. Drew Weissman. Every day, they bumped into each other at the copy machine. And every day, he saw her careful notes and precise measurements. He noticed her perfect data and marveled at her focus and persistence. The more they talked, the more excited Dr. Weissman became about Kati's fresh new ideas.

Kati felt her shoulders unclench. Finally, someone was listening. She was so close to success she could almost feel it swirling in the air around her.

The snowy Philadelphia haze gave way to a warm, sunny spring, and still Kati pressed on.

In every experiment, her messenger RNA vaccines caused an immune reaction within the cell. It was fighting off the vaccines as if they were *invaders* instead of *helpers*. This was a huge problem.

Kati tried adding different compounds to the mixture to stop the reaction, but nothing seemed to work. Then she made an important discovery. When she added a certain chemical—pseudouridine—the messages made it through.

A thousand thoughts flooded Kati's mind at once. This was the breakthrough she'd been waiting for.

She and Dr. Weissman quickly published their findings in a scientific journal and applied for more funding to speed up their research.

But every company they asked turned them down.

"TOO STRANGE!"

"TOO NEW!"

"TOO DIFFERENT!"

And even more trouble lay ahead—news that was about to change their lives forever.

Near the end of 2019, a strong, new coronavirus began spreading across the globe. Within just a few weeks, every nation, large and small, was facing a dangerous pandemic. It was hard to predict who would survive this disease and who would not.

Countries everywhere shut down completely.

No work.

No school.

Empty store shelves.

Every family alone at home,
waiting for a miracle.
It was frightening and
almost unbelievable.
But it was really happening.

Suddenly, Kati's work was at the center of an international emergency. Almost *every* drug company wanted to create an mRNA vaccine—to prevent this new illness called COVID-19.

With more than thirty-five years of experience, mounds of research, and thousands of lab experiments behind her, Kati was ready.

But vaccines usually take many years to develop. And COVID-19 was spreading fast. It rolled through large urban areas like Paris, Rome, and New York City and whipped through tiny rural towns like wildfire. Many people died. Others waited outside hospitals, worried their loved ones might die before a vaccine could be created.

But they did not know about the fierce determination of Dr. Katalin Karikó.

Kati's team slipped on special protective suits and masked up. They stepped into the lab and got to work creating an mRNA mixture. Kati's message to human cells? Make fighter antibodies to destroy the invasive coronavirus.

To some, it seemed too fast, too new, too good
to be true—but Kati had been preparing for this
moment her entire life. Working around the clock,
her team had a vaccine ready the next day.

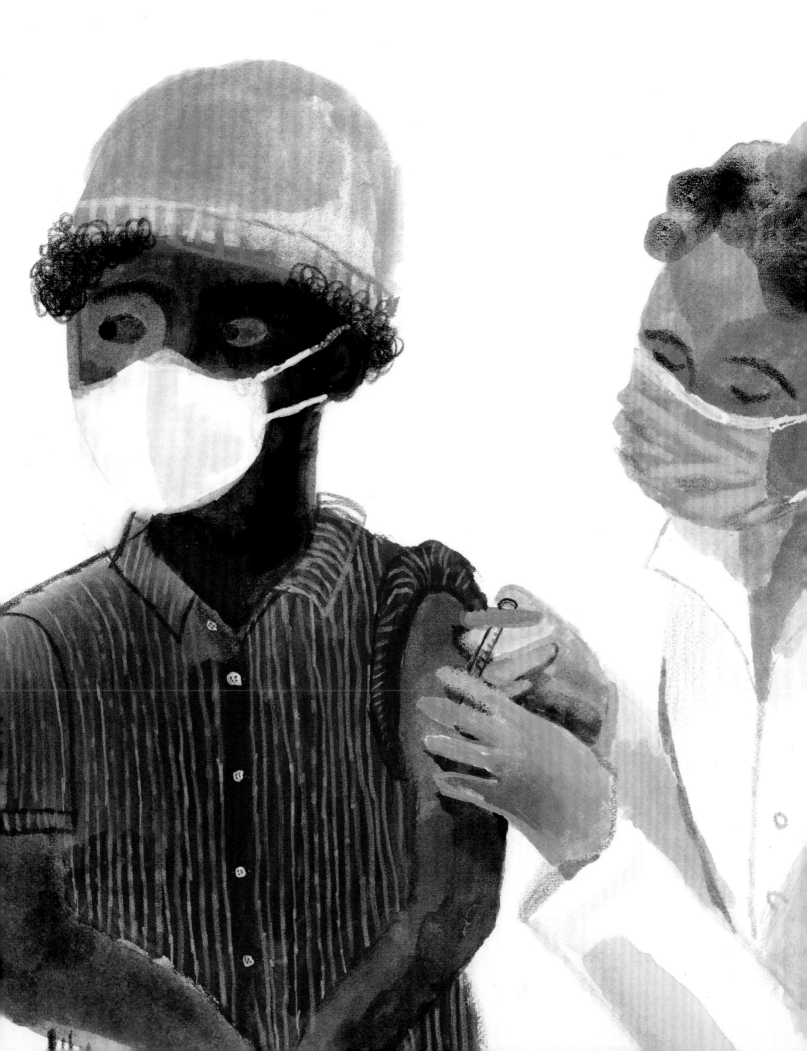

Now the vaccine needed to be tested and proven. Thousands of brave volunteers stepped forward and rolled up their sleeves. The first tiny messengers surged through their bodies, teaching their cells how to recognize a coronavirus spike protein so they could stomp it out.

There was nothing left to do but wait for the final test results to come in on November 8, 2020.

Days, weeks, and months ticked by. The volunteers faced a battery of tests to determine whether their bodies had created virus-fighting antibodies and special T cells that would remember how to fight off the coronavirus in the future.

Each day, Kati waited eagerly by the phone, hoping with all her heart that her vaccine worked.

Then she got the call.

Kati steadied her nerves and picked up her phone. *No matter what happens, she thought, I will never give up. I will keep working until we figure out how to beat this virus.*

"Hello?"

As Kati listened, joy flooded through her. She hung up the phone and pumped the air. She was so excited.

"It works!" she said. "I knew it would!" She ate a whole box of Goobers chocolate-covered peanuts to celebrate.

Reporters and camera crews raced to be the first to share the news. They clamored to interview Kati, and her photo appeared in articles around the world. She was suddenly famous. Hundreds of emails and phone calls flooded in. So many she couldn't answer them all. But she did respond to every volunteer who received the vaccine during the clinical trial. She wanted to thank them personally.

Dr. Katalin Karikó and Dr. Drew Weissman lined up to get their first dose of the vaccine on December 18, 2020. When the other doctors and nurses in the room found out who they were, everyone clapped and cheered. Kati was so overwhelmed that she cried.

She had focused her entire life's work on sending tiny messages to the smallest cells, to teach them how to fight infections. Now this mRNA technology could be used to fight all sorts of illnesses. The possibilities were endless.

Best of all, Kati knew that people all over the world would be able to fight the dreaded coronavirus and win the battle against COVID-19.

Because when Katalin Karikó made a decision, she stuck with it.

MORE ABOUT THE SCIENCE BEHIND THE COVID-19 VACCINE

Dear Reader,

I grew up in a small town in Hungary, in a house with no running water. How did I go from that life to impacting so many people with my scientific discoveries?

I can answer that question in one word: curiosity!

I have always been a curious girl. I spent a lot of time outside when I was young, and one day I was able to watch the neighbor's cow give birth. I was awestruck! From that moment on, I wanted to learn more about how the insides of living beings function. Curiosity and passion for how our bodies work washed over me, and I dove deep into studying it.

Later, when I was in college, I fixed my mind on biochemistry and all the possibilities of mRNA—that's short for messenger ribonucleic acid. It became my life's work. Still curious and driven forward by an urge to know and understand how to cure diseases, my thoughts whirled. I knew mRNA could tell the body to fight viruses like the coronavirus. But maybe it could also tell the heart how to make more healthy cells after a heart attack or correct the mutations in a cancerous tumor. The possibilities were endless! But thirty years ago, or even ten years ago, this all still sounded like science fiction to most people. It was hard to convince them otherwise.

We never expected our discovery to impact billions of people around the world, and not every idea will do that. But I want you to know that no matter what the people around you say, no matter how many people tell you what you are trying to do is impossible, you just keep on pursuing your dream. If you work hard to achieve your goals, you may impact a whole generation. But even if you impact only one person, you will have changed *their* world.

If you are a young girl who wants to become a scientist, I have a special message just for you. Go for it! And don't let anything stand in your way. Dream big!

—Dr. Katalin Karikó

DNA and RNA—What are they?

You can think of DNA as a giant, living notebook that contains all the genetic codes for your body's systems. DNA is the genetic code that makes you YOU! It is so important that it is locked inside a safe storage facility deep within the nucleus, which is in the middle of every cell in your body. It's microscopic. Tiny. But powerful!

DNA can tell us where our ancestors came from. It can tell detectives which criminal committed a certain crime. When Dr. Karikó was in college, she became absolutely fascinated with the amazing abilities of this tiny double-helix molecule called DNA. She wanted to harness its power and use it to cure diseases. But was that even possible? That's where RNA comes in.

RNA (ribonucleic acid) is different from DNA (*deoxy*ribonucleic acid) in two key ways: One, it is a single strand of rope instead of a double strand. And two, since it is made of ribose instead of oxyribose, both types of sugars, it is a bit more reactionary. Think of it like a guard dog, always ready to take action and protect your cells and body from harm by sending a warning message: "Fight this intruder now!" A special enzyme copies the warning, and messenger RNA (mRNA) translates it and carries it outside the nucleus, where DNA cannot go.

The most important recent development in the study of mRNA has been what Dr. Karikó was working on for decades. She discovered a way to use mRNA to deliver a *specific* message to cells to create antibodies to fight viruses. And once it has done its important work teaching cells how to fight a virus, it disintegrates and disappears.

How mRNA vaccines work

To fight diseases with mRNA vaccines, first the vaccine is injected into the muscle of the upper arm.

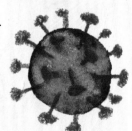

After that, immune cells learn from mRNA how to create special proteins to fight off future invaders. After they read the "message" and use it to create their virus-busting proteins, the immune cells destroy the message—sort of like how an old-time spy would read a secret message and then burn it.

The mRNA in the coronavirus vaccine teaches the cells how to make copies of what is called the spike protein. Those are the spikes that look like a crown on the outside of the coronavirus molecule. If a vaccinated person is exposed to the coronavirus in the future, the body will immediately notice and alert its master immune cells that have already been taught how to fight it off before it can cause any real damage.

How Dr. Karikó and Dr. Weissman got the message through

When Dr. Karikó and Dr. Weissman were performing their experiments, they used two groups of mice: One was given the mRNA vaccine, and the other was called a control group. A control group is not given the real medicine. That way, scientists can tell if a vaccine is working or not. The control group won't show any response, and the medicated group will.

But something amazing happened when Dr. Karikó and Dr. Weissman examined their control group of mice. They noticed that one of the proteins in their placebo injection had a soothing response. If they added this same protein, called pseudouridine (SOO-doh-yur-ih-DEEN), to the actual vaccine, it might help the message get through without causing an inflammation storm.

They tried it, and it worked!

Imagine for a moment if Dr. Karikó had given up on her dream of finding a way to get messages through to cells. We might never have developed a way to fight COVID-19, the disease caused by the coronavirus—and perhaps many more diseases in the future. Many thanks to our scientist hero, Dr. Katalin Karikó, for her perseverance and determination!

Other scientists who helped create the vaccine

Many other people helped develop this messenger RNA vaccine that began as a tiny dream in Dr. Karikó's mind—too many scientists to name, probably. But here are a few:

Professor **Zhang Yongzhen** and his team of scientists in China first studied the genetic sequence of the virus and bravely posted it publicly in January 2020. Without that information, a vaccine could not have been developed.

Dr. Barney Graham at the National Institutes of Health and **Dr. Jason McClellan** of the University of Texas at Austin worked to isolate the spike protein of the coronavirus from the mountains of genetic information that they received from the scientists in China.

The vaccines had to be encased in a lipid bubble (lipids are fats). This part was easy because scientists had been working on that for twenty-five years. Many thanks to all of them.

Cardiologist **Dr. Elliot Barnathan** hired Dr. Karikó as an assistant professor, even though the grant money that was supposed to be used to pay her never came in.

Neurosurgeon **Dr. David Langer** worked with Dr. Karikó in the lab and encouraged her not to give up. He said, "The best scientists try to prove themselves wrong. Kati's genius was a willingness to accept failure and keep trying, and her ability to answer questions people were not smart enough to ask. . . ."

Immunologist **Dr. Drew Weissman** worked closely with Dr. Karikó to develop the vaccine. He says they met because they frequently fought over the copy machine in their office. As they chatted while making copies of their work, they exchanged ideas.

TIMELINE

1955	Kati Karikó is born on January 17 in Szolnok, Hungary.
1960s	Kati attends school at Móricz Zsigmond Református Gimnázium in Kisújszállás, Hungary.
1978	Kati earns her bachelor's degree in biology from the University of Szeged in Szeged, Hungary.
1980	Kati Karikó and Bela Francia are married.
1982	Kati earns her doctorate in biochemistry from the University of Szeged and begins her research work there.
	Kati's daughter, Susan Francia, is born on November 8.
1985	Dr. Karikó and her family flee Hungary and arrive in the United States.
1989	Dr. Karikó joins the Perelman School of Medicine at the University of Pennsylvania and works with Dr. Elliott Barnathan, a cardiologist. After he leaves the university, Kati works with Dr. David Langer.
1997	Dr. Karikó begins collaborating with Dr. Drew Weissman.
2019	A new coronavirus is discovered in Wuhan, China, in November.
2020	Many scientists begin seeking an antidote and vaccine for this novel coronavirus. Dr. Karikó does more research and comes up with a vaccine to work against COVID-19.
	November 8—Susan's birthday—Dr. Karikó receives word that her vaccine works.
	Dr. Karikó and Dr. Weissman receive their first vaccinations on December 18.
2021	Pfizer BioNTech vaccine receives full FDA approval in August.
2021–22	Dr. Karikó receives numerous awards and prizes for her scientific achievements, including the prestigious Louisa Gross Horwitz Prize, the Breakthrough Prize in Life Sciences, and the Lasker-DeBakey Clinical Medical Research Award.

Dr. Karikó's daughter and the famous teddy bear

Dr. Karikó in the lab

SOURCES

Anderson, Bart R., Hiromi Muramatsu, Subba R. Nallagatla, Philip C. Bevilacqua, Lauren H. Sansing, Drew Weissman, and Katalin Karikó. "Incorporation of pseudouridine into mRNA enhances translation by diminishing PKR activation." *Nucleic Acids Research*, 38, no. 17 (September 1, 2010): 5884–5892. https://doi.org/10.1093/nar/gkq347.

"BioNTech's Karikó to be awarded honorary doctorate by University of Szeged." *Daily News Hungary*, January 27, 2021. https://dailynews hungary.com/biontechs-kariko-to-be-awarded-honorary-doctorate-by-university-of-szeged.

Campbell, Charlie. "Exclusive: The Chinese Scientist Who Sequenced the First COVID-19 Genome Speaks Out About the Controversies Surrounding His Work." *Time*, August 24, 2020. https://time.com/5882918/zhang-yongzhen-interview-china-coronavirus-genome.

"How mRNA COVID-19 Vaccines Work." Centers for Disease Control and Prevention. www.cdc.gov/coronavirus/2019-ncov/downloads /vaccines/COVID-19-mRNA-infographic_G_508.pdf.

Interviews with Dr. Katalin Karikó and daughter Susan Francia.

Kolata, Gina. "Kati Kariko Helped Shield the World from the Coronavirus." *New York Times*, April 8, 2021. www.nytimes.com/2021/04/08 /health/coronavirus-mrna-kariko.html.

Kollowee, Julie. "Covid Vaccine Technology Pioneer: 'I Never Doubted It Would Work.'" *Guardian*, November 21, 2020. https://www .theguardian.com/science/2020/nov/21/covid-vaccine-technology-pioneer-i-never-doubted-it-would-work.

Komaroff, Anthony L. "Why Are mRNA Vaccines So Exciting?" Harvard Health Publishing, November 1, 2021. www.health.harvard.edu/blog /why-are-mrna-vaccines-so-exciting-2020121021599#:~:text=The%20very%20first%20vaccines%20for,use%20in%20any%20disease.

"Messenger RNA (mRNA)." National Human Genome Research Institute, April 28, 2022. www.genome.gov/genetics-glossary/messenger-rna.

"Paving the Way for a COVID-19 Vaccine: A Conversation with Dr. Drew Weissman." Penn Medicine, 2022. www.pennmedicine.org/coronavirus /vaccine/qa-with-drew-weissman.

"Pfizer and BioNTech Announce Vaccine Candidate Against COVID-19 Achieved Success in First Interim Analysis from Phase 3 Study." Pfizer, November 9, 2020. www.pfizer.com/news/press-release/press-release-detail/pfizer-and-biontech-announce-vaccine-candidate-against.

"Research at the University of Szeged." University of Szeged, 2019. https://u-szeged.hu/hcemm/research-190517.

"Understanding mRNA COVID-19 Vaccines." Centers for Disease Control and Prevention, January 4, 2022. www.cdc.gov/coronavirus/2019-ncov /vaccines/different-vaccines/mrna.html.

To all the scientists who stuck with it, hour after long hour, day after day
and long into sleepless nights, and never saw success—your steadfast
determination in the face of failure is an inspiration to us all
—M.H.

To all the people who put themselves at risk to keep the
world going when it shut down in 2020
—V.M.

Quill Tree Books is an imprint of HarperCollins Publishers.

Kati's Tiny Messengers: Dr. Katalin Karikó and the Battle Against COVID-19
Text copyright © 2023 by Megan Hoyt
Illustrations copyright © 2023 by Vivien Mildenberger
Photos on p. 39 courtesy of Dr. Katalin Karikó

Library of Congress Control Number: 2023934234
ISBN 978-0-06-321662-4

The artist used mixed media to create the digittal illustrations for this book.
Typography by Rachel Zegar   23 24 25 26 27 RTLO 10 9 8 7 6 5 4 3 2 1   First Edition